369

MANIFESTATION

JOURNAL

THIS JOURNAL BELONGS TO:

_____

The Law of Attraction & Manifestation

Simply put, the Law of Attraction is the universal law that states any thoughts held within the mind can manifest into reality.

The thoughts in your mind are the concepts of goals and experiences that you would like to have in your life.

When you consistently hold these thoughts within your mind, you begin to attract and manifest these thoughts into reality.

This workbook will guide you in using the divine numbers of 3,6,9 and the law of attraction to help you manifest anything that you truly desire.

What is the 3,6,9 Manifestation Method?

"If you only knew the magnificence of the 3, 6 and 9, then you would have the key to the universe."

_____

Nikola Tesla

Nikola Tesla, one of history's greatest inventors (also the man whom Elon Musk named his car company after) recognized that the numbers 3, 6, and 9 had deep and powerful meaning. Tesla even considered them to be "divine numbers" with the Universe. Without diving too deep into the vortex of mathematics, let us look at examples of how the language of numbers connects to the Universe.

For instance, a circle has 360°, and adding these numbers individually (3+6+0-9) gives you 9. Splitting a circle in half gives you 180° (1 + 8 + 0 = 9), a quarter of a circle is 90° (9 + 0 = 9). 12 months in a year (1 + 2 = 3), 24 hours in a day (2 + 4 = 6). With these few examples, it is easy to see that numbers and mathematics play a mystical role and connection to the Universe.

Those that understand the harmonious relations to numbers and the Universe can tap into unlimited possibilities. With this knowledge, the divine numbers of 3,6, and 9 sets a perfect foundational method to manifesting anything that you truly desire into existence.

"If you want to find the secrets of the universe, think in terms of energy, frequency, and vibration" - Nikola Tesla

Without your voice,
we do not exist.
Please, support us and
leave an honest review on
Amazon

Just scan this QR code with
your phone's camera and
leave a review

HOW TO USE THIS JOURNAL:

Use affirmations to attract what you want and apply the 3,6,9 method. Check out the mindset activities and affirmation examples in the following pages for further guidance.

STEP 1:
Write down what you intend to manifest

STEP 2:
Write down your affirmation

Date 1/1/2023

I WANT TO MANIFEST: $10,000 Monthly Income

MY AFFIRMATION: I am a magnet for abundance and wealth.

3 AFFIRMATIONS IN THE MORNING

1	I am a magnet for abundance and wealth.
2	I am a magnet for abundance and wealth.
3	I am a magnet for abundance and wealth.

6 AFFIRMATIONS IN THE AFTERNOOON

1	I am a magnet for abundance and wealth.
2	I am a magnet for abundance and wealth.
3	I am a magnet for abundance and wealth.
4	I am a magnet for abundance and wealth.
5	I am a magnet for abundance and wealth.
6	I am a magnet for abundance and wealth.

9 AFFIRMATIONS IN EVENING

1	I am a magnet for abundance and wealth.
2	I am a magnet for abundance and wealth.
3	I am a magnet for abundance and wealth.
4	I am a magnet for abundance and wealth.
5	I am a magnet for abundance and wealth.
6	I am a magnet for abundance and wealth.
7	I am a magnet for abundance and wealth.
8	I am a magnet for abundance and wealth.
9	I am a magnet for abundance and wealth.

STEP 3:
Apply 3,6,9 Method by writing your affirmation: 3x's morning, 6x's afternoon, and 9 x's evening

Feel As If Game

To successfully manifest your desires, it is important that you get into the feeling as if you already have it. This game will help you get into the mindset of good feelings that you will experience once your desires manifest into your life.

1. Imagine that you have won the lottery and are guaranteed $200,000 every year for the rest of your life.

Start a timer for at least 60s and imagine all the good feelings flow through you. The longer you can go, the better.

Feel as if you received your first payment. How would that make you feel? How will this improve your life? What new things will you get to enjoy that you have not been able to experience?

2. Imagine the perfect romantic partner coming into your life, being in each other's arms, and loving each other deeply.

Start a timer for at least 60s and imagine all the good feelings flow through you.

Feel the deep connection and love that you have for one another. Feel the affection and loving energy that your partner pours out to you. Imagine the sweet and loving way that they talk to you. Feel how happy you are that they are in your life.

3. Imagine receiving news through a phone call that you just landed your dream job or huge business deal.

Start a timer for at least 60s and imagine all the good feelings flow through you.

Feel the overwhelming excitement and joy that you will feel once you hear this news. You share this news with friends and family and they tell you how proud they are of you and your accomplishments. How do you plan on celebrating?

4. Imagine suddenly being inspired by such a creative idea that could help so many people and positively make a difference in this world. This idea can easily become a reality.

Start a timer for at least 60s and imagine all the good feelings flow through you. The longer you can go, the better.

Feel the feelings of excitement and anticipation as this idea comes to you. Feel the ideas pouring out of you as you write them on paper. Feel the feeling of happiness and fulfillment for making a difference in this world.

5. Imagine that one thing you have always wanted to do but have been afraid or apprehensive to try out. Imagine that today is the day you finally have done it.

Start a timer for at least 60s and imagine all the good feelings flow through you.

Feel the sense of accomplishment and confidence that you have gained for doing it. Feel the feelings of being proud of yourself for overcoming your fears and doubts. To have pushed yourself outside of your comfort zone in order to grow and succeed.

6. Imagine looking into the mirror and feeling great! That you LOOK and FEEL extraordinary.

Start a timer for at least 60s and imagine all the good feelings flow through you.

Feel the feelings of love and gratitude that you have for yourself. Feel how great it is to have a big smile on your face as you appreciate and love your body right now.

LOVE AFFIRMATIONS

1. I am so happy and grateful that I have found the love of my life.

2. I am so happy to be in a healthy relationship

3. The Universe is sending me my soulmate.

4. I am attracting love.

5. I spread love and kindness everywhere I go.

6. I am manifesting love.

7. I am deeply loved by everyone around me.

8. I am making room for an amazing partner in my life.

9. My partner shows me deep, passionate love.

10. I am in a wonderful relationship with someone that treats me right.

11. I am overwhelmed with love!

12. I open my heart to love.

13. I am allowing the Universe to bring me, my true love.

14. I am in the healthiest relationship of my life.

15. I am in a mind-blowing, passionate, and romantic relationship.

16. I only attract healthy relationships.

17. I am attracting the perfect person for me.

18. I am in love with myself.

19. I am surrounded by love.

20. I am happy to give and receive love every day.

21. I am attracting real connection.

22. I am attracting a loving and affectionate partner.

23. I am grateful for the love in my life.

24. I am the vibration of love

25. I have the power to love no matter what.

WEALTH AFFIRMATIONS

1. I am worthy of being wealthy.

2. I am a magnet for being wealthy

3. Money comes to me in expected and unexpected ways.

4. I embrace new avenues of income.

5. Money comes to me easily and effortlessly.

6. I use money to better my life and the lives of others.

7. My finances improve beyond my dreams.

8. I constantly attract new opportunities that create more money.

9. I am able to handle large sums of money.

10. I can handle massive success with grace.

11. Money creates positive impacts in my life.

12. I am worthy of a wealthy life.

13. Money comes to me in miraculous ways.

14. I love my positive, happy, and abundant life.

15. The more I give, the more I receive. The more I receive, the more I give.

16. Money now comes to me in unexpected resources and I am grateful.

17. Money flows to me easily.

18. I am sensible with money and manage it wisely.

19. I allow my income to constantly expand and I always live in comfort and joy.

20. Every day I am attracting and saving more money every day.

21. I am debt-free and money is constantly flowing into my life.

22. Attracting money is easy.

23. I am fully supported in making money by doing what I love to do.

24. Whatever activities I perform make money for me.

25. My income exceeds my expenses.

HEALTH AFFIRMATIONS

1. I am healed, restored, and filled with vitality.

2. I am completely healthy now.

3. I am healthy, happy, and radiant.

4. I am loving and appreciating my body.

5. I am loving feeling fit and strong.

6. I am loving feeling energetic and vibrant.

7. I am loving feeling positive and optimistic.

8. I am loving feeling focused and clear.

9. I am conquering my illness; I am defeating it steadily each day.

10. I am sleeping deeply and peacefully.

11. I am loving and caring for my body and it is caring for me.

12. I am nourishing my body with plenty of water.

13. I am nourishing my body with fresh natural foods.

14. I am nourishing my body with movement and exercise.

15. I am nourishing my body with sunshine and fresh air.

16. I am nourishing my body with positive and healthy thoughts.

17. I am always making choices that are supportive of my health and well-being.

18. I am now surprising myself with how motivated I am to exercise.

19. I am free of stress.

20. I always make healthy choices.

21. I am grateful for the healing that is happening in my body.

22. Every day and every way, my body grows healthier and stronger.

23. I love my body and everything in it.

24. I enjoy eating the food that is best for my body.

25. My body heals itself easily and rapidly.

GENERAL AFFIRMATIONS

1. I can tap into a wellspring of inner happiness anytime I wish.

2. I have an active sense of humor and love to share laughter with others.

3. I rest in happiness when I go to sleep, knowing all is well in my world.

4. I look at the world around me and can't help but smile and feel joy.

5. I find joy and pleasure in the most simple things in life.

6. My heart is overflowing with joy.

7. I am a source of inspiration and motivation.

8. I bring joy and peace to others.

9. My best gift is my life.

10. I trust that my faith in the Universe will gift me with all that I need in life.

11. I am a magnet for positivity, abundance, and blessings.

12. I visualize my dream life and watch as it manifests into reality.

13. I am capable of doing anything that I set my mind on doing.

14. I radiate grace, charm, and beauty.

15. I am a blessing to the people in my life.

16. I am choosing this time to strengthen my faith in me.

17. I am born to do great things.

18. My positive attitude brings me success.

19. Everything that is happening now is happening for my ultimate good.

20. I posses the qualities needed to be extremely successful

21. I am successful and in alignment with my higher purpose.

22. I am excellent at what I do.

23. I am attracting my wildest dreams with ease and peace.

24. I can rest knowing all of my desires are coming to me.

25. Every day I discover interesting and exciting new paths to pursue.

Date _____

I WANT TO MANIFEST: _____

MY AFFIRMATION: _____

3 MORNING AFFIRMATIONS ☀

_____

_____

_____

6 AFTERNOON AFFIRMATIONS ☀

_____

_____

_____

_____

_____

_____

9 EVENING AFFIRMATIONS ☁

_____

_____

_____

_____

_____

_____

_____

_____

_____

Date _____

I WANT TO MANIFEST: _____

MY AFFIRMATION: _____

3 MORNING AFFIRMATIONS ☀

_____

_____

_____

6 AFTERNOON AFFIRMATIONS ☀

_____

_____

_____

_____

_____

_____

9 EVENING AFFIRMATIONS ☁

_____

_____

_____

_____

_____

_____

_____

_____

_____

Date _____

I WANT TO MANIFEST: _____

MY AFFIRMATION: _____

3 MORNING AFFIRMATIONS

_____

_____

_____

6 AFTERNOON AFFIRMATIONS

_____

_____

_____

_____

_____

_____

9 EVENING AFFIRMATIONS

_____

_____

_____

_____

_____

_____

_____

_____

_____

Date _____

I WANT TO MANIFEST: _____

MY AFFIRMATION: _____

3 MORNING AFFIRMATIONS ☀

_____

_____

_____

6 AFTERNOON AFFIRMATIONS ☀

_____

_____

_____

_____

_____

_____

9 EVENING AFFIRMATIONS ☁

_____

_____

_____

_____

_____

_____

_____

_____

_____

Date _____

I WANT TO MANIFEST: _____

MY AFFIRMATION: _____

3 MORNING AFFIRMATIONS ☀

_____

_____

_____

6 AFTERNOON AFFIRMATIONS ☀

_____

_____

_____

_____

_____

_____

9 EVENING AFFIRMATIONS ☾

_____

_____

_____

_____

_____

_____

_____

_____

_____

I WANT TO MANIFEST: _____

MY AFFIRMATION: _____

3 MORNING AFFIRMATIONS ☀

_____

_____

_____

6 AFTERNOON AFFIRMATIONS ☀

_____

_____

_____

_____

_____

_____

9 EVENING AFFIRMATIONS ☁

_____

_____

_____

_____

_____

_____

_____

_____

_____

Date _____

I WANT TO MANIFEST: _____

MY AFFIRMATION: _____

3 MORNING AFFIRMATIONS ☀

_____

_____

_____

6 AFTERNOON AFFIRMATIONS ☀

_____

_____

_____

_____

_____

_____

9 EVENING AFFIRMATIONS ☁

_____

_____

_____

_____

_____

_____

_____

_____

_____

Date _____

I WANT TO MANIFEST: _____

MY AFFIRMATION: _____

3 MORNING AFFIRMATIONS ☀

_____

_____

_____

6 AFTERNOON AFFIRMATIONS ☀

_____

_____

_____

_____

_____

_____

9 EVENING AFFIRMATIONS ☁

_____

_____

_____

_____

_____

_____

_____

_____

_____

Date _____

I WANT TO MANIFEST: _____

MY AFFIRMATION: _____

3 MORNING AFFIRMATIONS ☀

_____

_____

_____

6 AFTERNOON AFFIRMATIONS ☀

_____

_____

_____

_____

_____

_____

9 EVENING AFFIRMATIONS ☁

_____

_____

_____

_____

_____

_____

_____

_____

_____

Date _____

I WANT TO MANIFEST: _____

MY AFFIRMATION: _____

3 MORNING AFFIRMATIONS ☀

_____

_____

_____

6 AFTERNOON AFFIRMATIONS ☀

_____

_____

_____

_____

_____

_____

9 EVENING AFFIRMATIONS ☾

_____

_____

_____

_____

_____

_____

_____

_____

_____

Date _____

I WANT TO MANIFEST: _____

MY AFFIRMATION: _____

3 MORNING AFFIRMATIONS ☀

_____

_____

_____

6 AFTERNOON AFFIRMATIONS ☼

_____

_____

_____

_____

_____

_____

9 EVENING AFFIRMATIONS ☁

_____

_____

_____

_____

_____

_____

_____

_____

_____

Date _____

I WANT TO MANIFEST: _____

MY AFFIRMATION: _____

3 MORNING AFFIRMATIONS ☀

_____

_____

_____

6 AFTERNOON AFFIRMATIONS ☀

_____

_____

_____

_____

_____

_____

9 EVENING AFFIRMATIONS ☁

_____

_____

_____

_____

_____

_____

_____

_____

_____

Date _____

I WANT TO MANIFEST: _____

MY AFFIRMATION: _____

3 MORNING AFFIRMATIONS ☀

_____
_____
_____

6 AFTERNOON AFFIRMATIONS ☀

_____
_____
_____
_____
_____
_____

9 EVENING AFFIRMATIONS ☁

_____
_____
_____
_____
_____
_____
_____
_____
_____

Date _____

I WANT TO MANIFEST: _____

MY AFFIRMATION: _____

3 MORNING AFFIRMATIONS ☀

_____

_____

_____

6 AFTERNOON AFFIRMATIONS ☼

_____

_____

_____

_____

_____

_____

9 EVENING AFFIRMATIONS ☁

_____

_____

_____

_____

_____

_____

_____

_____

_____

Date _____

I WANT TO MANIFEST: _____

MY AFFIRMATION: _____

3 MORNING AFFIRMATIONS ☼

_____

_____

_____

6 AFTERNOON AFFIRMATIONS ☀

_____

_____

_____

_____

_____

_____

9 EVENING AFFIRMATIONS ☁

_____

_____

_____

_____

_____

_____

_____

_____

_____

I WANT TO MANIFEST: _____

MY AFFIRMATION: _____

3 MORNING AFFIRMATIONS ☀

_____

_____

_____

6 AFTERNOON AFFIRMATIONS ☀

_____

_____

_____

_____

_____

_____

9 EVENING AFFIRMATIONS ☾

_____

_____

_____

_____

_____

_____

_____

_____

_____

Date _____

I WANT TO MANIFEST: _____

MY AFFIRMATION: _____

3 MORNING AFFIRMATIONS ☀

_____

_____

_____

6 AFTERNOON AFFIRMATIONS ☀

_____

_____

_____

_____

_____

_____

9 EVENING AFFIRMATIONS ☁

_____

_____

_____

_____

_____

_____

_____

_____

_____

Date _____

I WANT TO MANIFEST: _____

MY AFFIRMATION: _____

3 MORNING AFFIRMATIONS ☀

_____

_____

_____

6 AFTERNOON AFFIRMATIONS ☀

_____

_____

_____

_____

_____

_____

9 EVENING AFFIRMATIONS ☁

_____

_____

_____

_____

_____

_____

_____

_____

_____

Date _____

I WANT TO MANIFEST: _____

MY AFFIRMATION: _____

3 MORNING AFFIRMATIONS ☀

_____

_____

_____

6 AFTERNOON AFFIRMATIONS ☀

_____

_____

_____

_____

_____

_____

9 EVENING AFFIRMATIONS ☁

_____

_____

_____

_____

_____

_____

_____

_____

_____

I WANT TO MANIFEST: _____

MY AFFIRMATION: _____

3 MORNING AFFIRMATIONS ☀

_____

_____

_____

6 AFTERNOON AFFIRMATIONS ☀

_____

_____

_____

_____

_____

_____

9 EVENING AFFIRMATIONS ☁

_____

_____

_____

_____

_____

_____

_____

_____

_____

Date _____

I WANT TO MANIFEST: _____

MY AFFIRMATION: _____

3 MORNING AFFIRMATIONS ☀

_____
_____
_____

6 AFTERNOON AFFIRMATIONS ☀

_____
_____
_____
_____
_____
_____

9 EVENING AFFIRMATIONS ☁

_____
_____
_____
_____
_____
_____
_____
_____
_____

Date _____

I WANT TO MANIFEST: _____

MY AFFIRMATION: _____

3 MORNING AFFIRMATIONS ☼

_____

_____

_____

6 AFTERNOON AFFIRMATIONS ☼

_____

_____

_____

_____

_____

_____

9 EVENING AFFIRMATIONS ☁

_____

_____

_____

_____

_____

_____

_____

_____

_____

Date _____

I WANT TO MANIFEST: _____

MY AFFIRMATION: _____

3 MORNING AFFIRMATIONS ☀

_____

_____

_____

6 AFTERNOON AFFIRMATIONS ☀

_____

_____

_____

_____

_____

_____

9 EVENING AFFIRMATIONS ☁

_____

_____

_____

_____

_____

_____

_____

_____

_____

Date _____

I WANT TO MANIFEST: _____

MY AFFIRMATION: _____

3 MORNING AFFIRMATIONS ☼

_____

_____

_____

6 AFTERNOON AFFIRMATIONS ☼

_____

_____

_____

_____

_____

_____

9 EVENING AFFIRMATIONS ☾

_____

_____

_____

_____

_____

_____

_____

_____

_____

Date _____

I WANT TO MANIFEST: _____

MY AFFIRMATION: _____

3 MORNING AFFIRMATIONS ☀

_____

_____

_____

6 AFTERNOON AFFIRMATIONS ☀

_____

_____

_____

_____

_____

_____

9 EVENING AFFIRMATIONS ☁

_____

_____

_____

_____

_____

_____

_____

_____

_____

Date _____

I WANT TO MANIFEST: _____

MY AFFIRMATION: _____

3 MORNING AFFIRMATIONS ☀

_____

_____

_____

6 AFTERNOON AFFIRMATIONS ☼

_____

_____

_____

_____

_____

_____

9 EVENING AFFIRMATIONS 🌙

_____

_____

_____

_____

_____

_____

_____

_____

_____

I WANT TO MANIFEST: _____

MY AFFIRMATION: _____

3 MORNING AFFIRMATIONS ☀

_____

_____

_____

6 AFTERNOON AFFIRMATIONS ☀

_____

_____

_____

_____

_____

_____

9 EVENING AFFIRMATIONS ☁

_____

_____

_____

_____

_____

_____

_____

_____

_____

Date _____

I WANT TO MANIFEST: _____

MY AFFIRMATION: _____

3 MORNING AFFIRMATIONS ☀

_____

_____

_____

6 AFTERNOON AFFIRMATIONS ☀

_____

_____

_____

_____

_____

_____

9 EVENING AFFIRMATIONS ☁

_____

_____

_____

_____

_____

_____

_____

_____

_____

Date _____

I WANT TO MANIFEST: _____

MY AFFIRMATION: _____

3 MORNING AFFIRMATIONS ☀

_____

_____

_____

6 AFTERNOON AFFIRMATIONS ☀

_____

_____

_____

_____

_____

_____

9 EVENING AFFIRMATIONS ☁

_____

_____

_____

_____

_____

_____

_____

_____

_____

Date _____

I WANT TO MANIFEST: _____

MY AFFIRMATION: _____

3 MORNING AFFIRMATIONS ☼

_____

_____

_____

6 AFTERNOON AFFIRMATIONS ☼

_____

_____

_____

_____

_____

_____

9 EVENING AFFIRMATIONS ☽

_____

_____

_____

_____

_____

_____

_____

_____

_____

I WANT TO MANIFEST: _____

MY AFFIRMATION: _____

3 MORNING AFFIRMATIONS ☀

_____

_____

_____

6 AFTERNOON AFFIRMATIONS ☼

_____

_____

_____

_____

_____

_____

9 EVENING AFFIRMATIONS ☁

_____

_____

_____

_____

_____

_____

_____

_____

_____

Date _____

I WANT TO MANIFEST: _____

MY AFFIRMATION: _____

3 MORNING AFFIRMATIONS ☀

_____

_____

_____

6 AFTERNOON AFFIRMATIONS ☀

_____

_____

_____

_____

_____

_____

9 EVENING AFFIRMATIONS ☁

_____

_____

_____

_____

_____

_____

_____

_____

_____

Date _____

I WANT TO MANIFEST: _____

MY AFFIRMATION: _____

3 MORNING AFFIRMATIONS ☀

_____

_____

_____

6 AFTERNOON AFFIRMATIONS ☼

_____

_____

_____

_____

_____

_____

9 EVENING AFFIRMATIONS ☁

_____

_____

_____

_____

_____

_____

_____

_____

_____

Date _____

I WANT TO MANIFEST: _____

MY AFFIRMATION: _____

3 MORNING AFFIRMATIONS ☀

_____

_____

_____

6 AFTERNOON AFFIRMATIONS ☼

_____

_____

_____

_____

_____

9 EVENING AFFIRMATIONS ☁

_____

_____

_____

_____

_____

_____

_____

Date _____

I WANT TO MANIFEST: _____

MY AFFIRMATION: _____

3 MORNING AFFIRMATIONS ☼

_____

_____

_____

6 AFTERNOON AFFIRMATIONS ☼

_____

_____

_____

_____

_____

_____

9 EVENING AFFIRMATIONS ☁

_____

_____

_____

_____

_____

_____

_____

_____

_____

Date _____

I WANT TO MANIFEST: _____

MY AFFIRMATION: _____

3 MORNING AFFIRMATIONS ☀

_____

_____

_____

6 AFTERNOON AFFIRMATIONS ☀

_____

_____

_____

_____

_____

_____

9 EVENING AFFIRMATIONS ☁

_____

_____

_____

_____

_____

_____

_____

_____

_____

Date _____

I WANT TO MANIFEST: _____

MY AFFIRMATION: _____

3 MORNING AFFIRMATIONS ☀

_____

_____

_____

6 AFTERNOON AFFIRMATIONS ☀

_____

_____

_____

_____

_____

_____

9 EVENING AFFIRMATIONS ☾

_____

_____

_____

_____

_____

_____

_____

_____

_____

Date _____

I WANT TO MANIFEST: _____

MY AFFIRMATION: _____

3 MORNING AFFIRMATIONS ☀

_____

_____

_____

6 AFTERNOON AFFIRMATIONS ☀

_____

_____

_____

_____

_____

_____

9 EVENING AFFIRMATIONS ☾

_____

_____

_____

_____

_____

_____

_____

_____

_____

Date _____

I WANT TO MANIFEST: _____

MY AFFIRMATION: _____

3 MORNING AFFIRMATIONS ☀

_____

_____

_____

6 AFTERNOON AFFIRMATIONS ☼

_____

_____

_____

_____

_____

_____

9 EVENING AFFIRMATIONS ☁

_____

_____

_____

_____

_____

_____

_____

_____

_____

Date _____

I WANT TO MANIFEST: _____

MY AFFIRMATION: _____

3 MORNING AFFIRMATIONS ☀

_____

_____

_____

6 AFTERNOON AFFIRMATIONS ☀

_____

_____

_____

_____

_____

_____

9 EVENING AFFIRMATIONS ☁

_____

_____

_____

_____

_____

_____

_____

_____

_____

I WANT TO MANIFEST: _____

MY AFFIRMATION: _____

3 MORNING AFFIRMATIONS ☀

_____

_____

_____

6 AFTERNOON AFFIRMATIONS ☀

_____

_____

_____

_____

_____

_____

9 EVENING AFFIRMATIONS ☾

_____

_____

_____

_____

_____

_____

_____

_____

_____

Date _____

I WANT TO MANIFEST: _____

MY AFFIRMATION: _____

3 MORNING AFFIRMATIONS ☀

_____

_____

_____

6 AFTERNOON AFFIRMATIONS ☀

_____

_____

_____

_____

_____

_____

9 EVENING AFFIRMATIONS ☁

_____

_____

_____

_____

_____

_____

_____

_____

_____

Date _____

I WANT TO MANIFEST: _____

MY AFFIRMATION: _____

3 MORNING AFFIRMATIONS ☀

_____

_____

_____

6 AFTERNOON AFFIRMATIONS ☀

_____

_____

_____

_____

_____

_____

9 EVENING AFFIRMATIONS ☁

_____

_____

_____

_____

_____

_____

_____

_____

_____

Date _____

I WANT TO MANIFEST: _____

MY AFFIRMATION: _____

3 MORNING AFFIRMATIONS ☀

_____

_____

_____

6 AFTERNOON AFFIRMATIONS ☀

_____

_____

_____

_____

_____

_____

9 EVENING AFFIRMATIONS ☁

_____

_____

_____

_____

_____

_____

_____

_____

_____

Date _____

I WANT TO MANIFEST: _____

MY AFFIRMATION: _____

3 MORNING AFFIRMATIONS ☼

_____

_____

_____

6 AFTERNOON AFFIRMATIONS ☼

_____

_____

_____

_____

_____

_____

9 EVENING AFFIRMATIONS ☁

_____

_____

_____

_____

_____

_____

_____

_____

_____

Date _____

I WANT TO MANIFEST: _____

MY AFFIRMATION: _____

3 MORNING AFFIRMATIONS ☀

_____

_____

_____

6 AFTERNOON AFFIRMATIONS ☼

_____

_____

_____

_____

_____

_____

9 EVENING AFFIRMATIONS ☁

_____

_____

_____

_____

_____

_____

_____

_____

_____

Date _____

I WANT TO MANIFEST: _____

MY AFFIRMATION: _____

3 MORNING AFFIRMATIONS ☀

_____

_____

_____

6 AFTERNOON AFFIRMATIONS ☀

_____

_____

_____

_____

_____

_____

9 EVENING AFFIRMATIONS ☁

_____

_____

_____

_____

_____

_____

_____

_____

_____

Date _____

I WANT TO MANIFEST: _____

MY AFFIRMATION: _____

3 MORNING AFFIRMATIONS ☀

_____

_____

_____

6 AFTERNOON AFFIRMATIONS ☼

_____

_____

_____

_____

_____

_____

9 EVENING AFFIRMATIONS ☁

_____

_____

_____

_____

_____

_____

_____

_____

_____

Date _____

I WANT TO MANIFEST: _____

MY AFFIRMATION: _____

3 MORNING AFFIRMATIONS ☀

_____

_____

_____

6 AFTERNOON AFFIRMATIONS ☀

_____

_____

_____

_____

_____

_____

9 EVENING AFFIRMATIONS ☁

_____

_____

_____

_____

_____

_____

_____

_____

_____

Date _____

I WANT TO MANIFEST: _____

MY AFFIRMATION: _____

3 MORNING AFFIRMATIONS ☀

_____

_____

_____

6 AFTERNOON AFFIRMATIONS ☀

_____

_____

_____

_____

_____

9 EVENING AFFIRMATIONS ☁

_____

_____

_____

_____

_____

_____

_____

Date _____

I WANT TO MANIFEST: _____

MY AFFIRMATION: _____

3 MORNING AFFIRMATIONS ☀

_____

_____

_____

6 AFTERNOON AFFIRMATIONS ☀

_____

_____

_____

_____

_____

_____

9 EVENING AFFIRMATIONS ☁

_____

_____

_____

_____

_____

_____

_____

_____

_____

I WANT TO MANIFEST: _____

MY AFFIRMATION: _____

3 MORNING AFFIRMATIONS ☀

_____

_____

_____

6 AFTERNOON AFFIRMATIONS ☼

_____

_____

_____

_____

_____

_____

9 EVENING AFFIRMATIONS ☁

_____

_____

_____

_____

_____

_____

_____

_____

_____

Date _____

I WANT TO MANIFEST: _____

MY AFFIRMATION: _____

3 MORNING AFFIRMATIONS ☀

_____

_____

_____

6 AFTERNOON AFFIRMATIONS ☀

_____

_____

_____

_____

_____

_____

9 EVENING AFFIRMATIONS ☾

_____

_____

_____

_____

_____

_____

_____

_____

_____

I WANT TO MANIFEST: _____

MY AFFIRMATION: _____

3 MORNING AFFIRMATIONS ☀

_____

_____

_____

6 AFTERNOON AFFIRMATIONS ☀

_____

_____

_____

_____

_____

_____

9 EVENING AFFIRMATIONS ☁

_____

_____

_____

_____

_____

_____

_____

_____

Date _____

I WANT TO MANIFEST: _____

MY AFFIRMATION: _____

3 MORNING AFFIRMATIONS ☀

_____

_____

_____

6 AFTERNOON AFFIRMATIONS ☀

_____

_____

_____

_____

_____

_____

9 EVENING AFFIRMATIONS ☁

_____

_____

_____

_____

_____

_____

_____

_____

_____

Date _____

I WANT TO MANIFEST: _____

MY AFFIRMATION: _____

3 MORNING AFFIRMATIONS ☼

_____

_____

_____

6 AFTERNOON AFFIRMATIONS ☼

_____

_____

_____

_____

_____

_____

9 EVENING AFFIRMATIONS ☁

_____

_____

_____

_____

_____

_____

_____

_____

_____

Date _____

I WANT TO MANIFEST: _____

MY AFFIRMATION: _____

3 MORNING AFFIRMATIONS ☀

_____

_____

_____

6 AFTERNOON AFFIRMATIONS ☀

_____

_____

_____

_____

_____

_____

9 EVENING AFFIRMATIONS ☽

_____

_____

_____

_____

_____

_____

_____

_____

_____

Date _____

I WANT TO MANIFEST: _____

MY AFFIRMATION: _____

3 MORNING AFFIRMATIONS

_____

_____

_____

6 AFTERNOON AFFIRMATIONS

_____

_____

_____

_____

_____

_____

9 EVENING AFFIRMATIONS

_____

_____

_____

_____

_____

_____

_____

_____

_____

Date _____

I WANT TO MANIFEST: _____

MY AFFIRMATION: _____

3 MORNING AFFIRMATIONS ☀

_____

_____

_____

6 AFTERNOON AFFIRMATIONS ☀

_____

_____

_____

_____

_____

_____

9 EVENING AFFIRMATIONS ☁

_____

_____

_____

_____

_____

_____

_____

_____

_____

I WANT TO MANIFEST: _____

MY AFFIRMATION: _____

3 MORNING AFFIRMATIONS ☀

_____

_____

_____

6 AFTERNOON AFFIRMATIONS ☀

_____

_____

_____

_____

_____

_____

9 EVENING AFFIRMATIONS ☁

_____

_____

_____

_____

_____

_____

_____

_____

_____

Date _____

I WANT TO MANIFEST: _____

MY AFFIRMATION: _____

3 MORNING AFFIRMATIONS ☀

_____

_____

_____

6 AFTERNOON AFFIRMATIONS ☀

_____

_____

_____

_____

_____

_____

9 EVENING AFFIRMATIONS ☁

_____

_____

_____

_____

_____

_____

_____

_____

_____

Date _____

I WANT TO MANIFEST: _____

MY AFFIRMATION: _____

3 MORNING AFFIRMATIONS ☀

_____

_____

_____

6 AFTERNOON AFFIRMATIONS ☀

_____

_____

_____

_____

_____

_____

9 EVENING AFFIRMATIONS ☁

_____

_____

_____

_____

_____

_____

_____

_____

_____

Date _____

I WANT TO MANIFEST: _____

MY AFFIRMATION: _____

3 MORNING AFFIRMATIONS ☀

_____

_____

_____

6 AFTERNOON AFFIRMATIONS ☀

_____

_____

_____

_____

_____

_____

9 EVENING AFFIRMATIONS ☁

_____

_____

_____

_____

_____

_____

_____

_____

_____

I WANT TO MANIFEST: _____

MY AFFIRMATION: _____

3 MORNING AFFIRMATIONS ☀

_____

_____

_____

6 AFTERNOON AFFIRMATIONS ☀

_____

_____

_____

_____

_____

_____

9 EVENING AFFIRMATIONS ☁

_____

_____

_____

_____

_____

_____

_____

_____

_____

Date _____

I WANT TO MANIFEST: _____

MY AFFIRMATION: _____

3 MORNING AFFIRMATIONS ☀

_____

_____

_____

6 AFTERNOON AFFIRMATIONS ☀

_____

_____

_____

_____

_____

_____

9 EVENING AFFIRMATIONS ☁

_____

_____

_____

_____

_____

_____

_____

_____

_____

Date _____

I WANT TO MANIFEST: _____

MY AFFIRMATION: _____

3 MORNING AFFIRMATIONS ☀

_____

_____

_____

6 AFTERNOON AFFIRMATIONS ☼

_____

_____

_____

_____

_____

_____

9 EVENING AFFIRMATIONS 🌙

_____

_____

_____

_____

_____

_____

_____

_____

_____

Date _____

I WANT TO MANIFEST: _____

MY AFFIRMATION: _____

3 MORNING AFFIRMATIONS ☀

_____

_____

_____

6 AFTERNOON AFFIRMATIONS ☀

_____

_____

_____

_____

_____

_____

9 EVENING AFFIRMATIONS ☁

_____

_____

_____

_____

_____

_____

_____

_____

_____

Date _____

I WANT TO MANIFEST: _____

MY AFFIRMATION: _____

3 MORNING AFFIRMATIONS ☀

_____

_____

_____

6 AFTERNOON AFFIRMATIONS ☀

_____

_____

_____

_____

_____

_____

9 EVENING AFFIRMATIONS ☁

_____

_____

_____

_____

_____

_____

_____

_____

_____

Date _____

I WANT TO MANIFEST: _____

MY AFFIRMATION: _____

3 MORNING AFFIRMATIONS ☀

_____

_____

_____

6 AFTERNOON AFFIRMATIONS ☀

_____

_____

_____

_____

_____

_____

9 EVENING AFFIRMATIONS ☁

_____

_____

_____

_____

_____

_____

_____

_____

_____

Date _____

I WANT TO MANIFEST: _____

MY AFFIRMATION: _____

3 MORNING AFFIRMATIONS ☀

_____

_____

_____

6 AFTERNOON AFFIRMATIONS ☀

_____

_____

_____

_____

_____

_____

9 EVENING AFFIRMATIONS ☁

_____

_____

_____

_____

_____

_____

_____

_____

_____

I WANT TO MANIFEST: _____

MY AFFIRMATION: _____

3 MORNING AFFIRMATIONS ☀

_____

_____

_____

6 AFTERNOON AFFIRMATIONS ☀

_____

_____

_____

_____

_____

_____

9 EVENING AFFIRMATIONS ☁

_____

_____

_____

_____

_____

_____

_____

_____

_____

I WANT TO MANIFEST: _____

MY AFFIRMATION: _____

3 MORNING AFFIRMATIONS ☀

_____

_____

_____

6 AFTERNOON AFFIRMATIONS ☼

_____

_____

_____

_____

_____

_____

9 EVENING AFFIRMATIONS ☁

_____

_____

_____

_____

_____

_____

_____

_____

_____

Date _____

I WANT TO MANIFEST: _____

MY AFFIRMATION: _____

3 MORNING AFFIRMATIONS ☀

_____

_____

_____

6 AFTERNOON AFFIRMATIONS ☀

_____

_____

_____

_____

_____

_____

9 EVENING AFFIRMATIONS ☁

_____

_____

_____

_____

_____

_____

_____

_____

_____

Date _____

I WANT TO MANIFEST: _____

MY AFFIRMATION: _____

3 MORNING AFFIRMATIONS ☀

_____

_____

_____

6 AFTERNOON AFFIRMATIONS ☀

_____

_____

_____

_____

_____

_____

9 EVENING AFFIRMATIONS ☾

_____

_____

_____

_____

_____

_____

_____

_____

_____

Date _____

I WANT TO MANIFEST: _____

MY AFFIRMATION: _____

3 MORNING AFFIRMATIONS ☀

_____

_____

_____

6 AFTERNOON AFFIRMATIONS ☀

_____

_____

_____

_____

_____

_____

9 EVENING AFFIRMATIONS ☁

_____

_____

_____

_____

_____

_____

_____

_____

_____

Date _____

I WANT TO MANIFEST: _____

MY AFFIRMATION: _____

3 MORNING AFFIRMATIONS ☀

_____

_____

_____

6 AFTERNOON AFFIRMATIONS ☀

_____

_____

_____

_____

_____

_____

9 EVENING AFFIRMATIONS ☁

_____

_____

_____

_____

_____

_____

_____

_____

_____

Date _____

I WANT TO MANIFEST: _____

MY AFFIRMATION: _____

3 MORNING AFFIRMATIONS ☀

_____

_____

_____

6 AFTERNOON AFFIRMATIONS ☀

_____

_____

_____

_____

_____

_____

9 EVENING AFFIRMATIONS ☾

_____

_____

_____

_____

_____

_____

_____

_____

_____

Date _____

I WANT TO MANIFEST: _____

MY AFFIRMATION: _____

3 MORNING AFFIRMATIONS ☀

_____

_____

_____

6 AFTERNOON AFFIRMATIONS ☀

_____

_____

_____

_____

_____

_____

9 EVENING AFFIRMATIONS ☁

_____

_____

_____

_____

_____

_____

_____

_____

_____

Date _____

I WANT TO MANIFEST: _____

MY AFFIRMATION: _____

3 MORNING AFFIRMATIONS ☀

_____

_____

_____

6 AFTERNOON AFFIRMATIONS ☀

_____

_____

_____

_____

_____

_____

9 EVENING AFFIRMATIONS ☁

_____

_____

_____

_____

_____

_____

_____

_____

_____

Date _____

I WANT TO MANIFEST: _____

MY AFFIRMATION: _____

3 MORNING AFFIRMATIONS ☀

_____

_____

_____

6 AFTERNOON AFFIRMATIONS ☼

_____

_____

_____

_____

_____

_____

9 EVENING AFFIRMATIONS ☁

_____

_____

_____

_____

_____

_____

_____

_____

_____

Date _____

I WANT TO MANIFEST: _____

MY AFFIRMATION: _____

3 MORNING AFFIRMATIONS ☀

_____

_____

_____

6 AFTERNOON AFFIRMATIONS ☼

_____

_____

_____

_____

_____

_____

9 EVENING AFFIRMATIONS ☁

_____

_____

_____

_____

_____

_____

_____

_____

_____

Date _____

I WANT TO MANIFEST: _____

MY AFFIRMATION: _____

3 MORNING AFFIRMATIONS ☀

_____

_____

_____

6 AFTERNOON AFFIRMATIONS ☀

_____

_____

_____

_____

_____

_____

9 EVENING AFFIRMATIONS ☾

_____

_____

_____

_____

_____

_____

_____

_____

_____

Date _____

I WANT TO MANIFEST: _____

MY AFFIRMATION: _____

3 MORNING AFFIRMATIONS ☀

_____

_____

_____

6 AFTERNOON AFFIRMATIONS ☀

_____

_____

_____

_____

_____

_____

9 EVENING AFFIRMATIONS ☁

_____

_____

_____

_____

_____

_____

_____

_____

_____

Date _____

I WANT TO MANIFEST: _____

MY AFFIRMATION: _____

3 MORNING AFFIRMATIONS ☀

_____

_____

_____

6 AFTERNOON AFFIRMATIONS ☼

_____

_____

_____

_____

_____

_____

9 EVENING AFFIRMATIONS ☁

_____

_____

_____

_____

_____

_____

_____

_____

_____

Date _____

I WANT TO MANIFEST: _____

MY AFFIRMATION: _____

3 MORNING AFFIRMATIONS ☀

_____

_____

_____

6 AFTERNOON AFFIRMATIONS ☀

_____

_____

_____

_____

_____

_____

9 EVENING AFFIRMATIONS ☁

_____

_____

_____

_____

_____

_____

_____

_____

_____

Date _____

I WANT TO MANIFEST: _____

MY AFFIRMATION: _____

3 MORNING AFFIRMATIONS ☀

_____

_____

_____

6 AFTERNOON AFFIRMATIONS ☼

_____

_____

_____

_____

_____

_____

9 EVENING AFFIRMATIONS ☁

_____

_____

_____

_____

_____

_____

_____

_____

_____

Date _____

I WANT TO MANIFEST: _____

MY AFFIRMATION: _____

3 MORNING AFFIRMATIONS ☀

_____

_____

_____

6 AFTERNOON AFFIRMATIONS ☀

_____

_____

_____

_____

_____

_____

9 EVENING AFFIRMATIONS ☽

_____

_____

_____

_____

_____

_____

_____

_____

_____

Date _____

I WANT TO MANIFEST: _____

MY AFFIRMATION: _____

3 MORNING AFFIRMATIONS ☀

_____

_____

_____

6 AFTERNOON AFFIRMATIONS ☀

_____

_____

_____

_____

_____

_____

9 EVENING AFFIRMATIONS ☁

_____

_____

_____

_____

_____

_____

_____

_____

_____

Date _____

I WANT TO MANIFEST: _____

MY AFFIRMATION: _____

3 MORNING AFFIRMATIONS ☀

_____

_____

_____

6 AFTERNOON AFFIRMATIONS ☀

_____

_____

_____

_____

_____

_____

9 EVENING AFFIRMATIONS ☁

_____

_____

_____

_____

_____

_____

_____

_____

_____

Date _____

I WANT TO MANIFEST: _____

MY AFFIRMATION: _____

3 MORNING AFFIRMATIONS ☀

_____

_____

_____

6 AFTERNOON AFFIRMATIONS ☀

_____

_____

_____

_____

_____

_____

9 EVENING AFFIRMATIONS ☾

_____

_____

_____

_____

_____

_____

_____

_____

_____

Date _____

I WANT TO MANIFEST: _____

MY AFFIRMATION: _____

3 MORNING AFFIRMATIONS

_____

_____

_____

6 AFTERNOON AFFIRMATIONS

_____

_____

_____

_____

_____

_____

9 EVENING AFFIRMATIONS

_____

_____

_____

_____

_____

_____

_____

_____

_____

Made in the USA
Las Vegas, NV
10 July 2023